To Carolyn
with since

Emily Dickinson

Judge Tenderly of Me

Judge Tenderly of Me

The Poems of Emily Dickinson

Selected and With an Afterword

by Winfield Townley Scott

Illustrated by Bill Greer

Hallmark Editions

Aside from several deliberate exceptions, the order of these poems is chronological, following the Dickinson editions by Thomas H. Johnson. The editor wishes also to acknowledge a debt of gratitude to Witter Bynner.   W.T.S.

Designed by Harald Peter.
Set in Trump Mediäval, a Venetian face designed by Professor Georg Trump, Munich.
Printed on Hallmark Eggshell Book paper.

Judge Tenderly of Me

THIS IS my letter to the World
That never wrote to Me—
The simple News that Nature told—
With tender Majesty

Her Message is committed
To Hands I cannot see—
For love of Her—Sweet—countrymen—
Judge tenderly—of Me

SUCCESS is counted sweetest
By those who ne'er succeed.
To comprehend a nectar
Requires sorest need.

Not one of all the purple Host
Who took the Flag today
Can tell the definition
So clear of Victory

As he defeated—dying—
On whose forbidden ear
The distant strains of triumph
Burst agonized and clear!

AN ALTERED look about the hills—
A Tyrian light the village fills—
A wider sunrise in the morn—
A deeper twilight on the lawn—
A print of a vermilion foot—
A purple finger on the slope—
A flippant fly upon the pane—
A spider at his trade again—
An added strut in Chanticleer—
A flower expected everywhere—
An axe shrill singing in the woods—
Fern odors on untravelled roads—
All this and more I cannot tell—
A furtive look you know as well—
And Nicodemus' Mystery
Receives its annual reply!

I SHOULD not dare to leave my friend,
Because—because if he should die
While I was gone—and I—too late—
Should reach the Heart that wanted me—

If I should disappoint the eyes
That hunted—hunted so—to see—
And could not bear to shut until
They "noticed" me—they noticed me—

If I should stab the patient faith
So sure I'd come—so sure I'd come—
It *listening*—listening—went to sleep—
Telling my tardy name—

My Heart would wish it broke before—
Since breaking then—since breaking then—
Were useless as next morning's sun—
Where midnight frosts—had lain!

THE MOUNTAINS stood in Haze—
The Valleys stopped below
And went or waited as they liked
The River and the Sky.

At leisure was the Sun—
His interests of Fire
A little from remark withdrawn—
The Twilight spoke the Spire,

So soft upon the Scene
The Act of evening fell
We felt how neighborly a Thing
Was the Invisible.

I TASTE a liquor never brewed—
From Tankards scooped in Pearl—
Not all the Vats upon the Rhine
Yield such an Alcohol!

Inebriate of Air—am I—
And Debauchee of Dew—
Reeling—thro endless summer days—
From inns of Molten Blue—

When "Landlords" turn the drunken Bee
Out of the Foxglove's door—
When Butterflies—renounce their "drams"—
I shall but drink the more!

Till Seraphs swing their snowy Hats—
And Saints—to windows run—
To see the little Tippler
Leaning against the—Sun—

SAFE IN their Alabaster Chambers—
Untouched by Morning—
And untouched by Noon—
Lie the meek members of the Resurrection—
Rafter of Satin—and Roof of Stone!

Grand go the Years—in the Crescent—
   above them—
Worlds scoop their Arcs—
And Firmaments—row—
Diadems—drop—and Doges—surrender—
Soundless as dots—on a Disc of Snow—

I FELT a Funeral, in my Brain,
And Mourners to and fro
Kept treading—treading—till it seemed
That Sense was breaking through—

And when they all were seated,
A Service, like a Drum—
Kept beating—beating—till I thought
My mind was going numb—

And then I heard them lift a Box
And creak across my Soul
With those same Boots of Lead, again,
Then Space—began to toll,

As all the Heavens were a Bell,
And Being, but an Ear,
And I, and Silence, some strange Race
Wrecked, solitary, here—

And then a Plank in Reason, broke,
And I dropped down, and down—
And hit a World, at every plunge,
And Finished knowing—then—

I'M NOBODY! Who are you?
Are you—Nobody—Too?
Then there's a pair of us?
Don't tell! they'd advertise—you know!

How dreary—to be—Somebody!
How public—like a Frog—
To tell one's name—the livelong June—
To an admiring Bog!

I KNOW some lonely Houses off the Road
A Robber'd like the look of—
Wooden barred,
And Windows hanging low,
Inviting to—
A Portico,
Where two could creep—
One—hand the Tools—
The other peep—
To make sure All's Asleep—
Old fashioned eyes—
Not easy to surprise!

How orderly the Kitchen'd look, by night,
With just a Clock—
But they could gag the Tick—
And Mice won't bark—
And so the Walls—don't tell—
None—will—

A pair of Spectacles ajar just stir—
An Almanac's aware—
Was it the Mat—winked,
Or a Nervous Star?
The Moon—slides down the stair,
To see who's there!

There's plunder—where—
Tankard, or Spoon—
Earring—or Stone—
A Watch—Some Ancient Brooch
To match the Grandmama—
Staid sleeping—there—

Day—rattles—too
Stealth's—slow—
The Sun has got as far
As the third Sycamore—
Screams Chanticleer
"Who's there"?

And Echoes—Trains away,
Sneer—"Where"!
While the old Couple, just astir,
Fancy the Sunrise—left the door ajar!

I GOT SO I could hear his name—
Without—Tremendous gain—
That Stop-sensation—on my Soul—
And Thunder—in the Room—

I got so I could walk across
That Angle in the floor,
Where he turned so, and I turned—how—
And all our Sinew tore—

I got so I could stir the Box—
In which his letters grew
Without that forcing, in my breath—
As Staples—driven through—

Could dimly recollect a Grace—
I think, they call it "God"—
Renowned to ease Extremity—
When Formula, had failed—

And shape my Hands—
Petition's way,
Tho' ignorant of a word
That Ordination—utters—

My Business, with the Cloud,
If any Power behind it, be,
Not subject to Despair—
It care, in some remoter way,
For so minute affair
As Misery—
Itself, too vast, for interrupting—more—

A BIRD came down the Walk—
He did not know I saw—
He bit an Angleworm in halves
And ate the fellow, raw,

And then he drank a Dew
From a convenient Grass—
And then hopped sidewise to the Wall
To let a Beetle pass—

He glanced with rapid eyes
That hurried all around—
They looked like frightened Beads, I thought—
He stirred his Velvet Head

Like one in danger, Cautious,
I offered him a Crumb
And he unrolled his feathers
And rowed him softer home—

Than Oars divide the Ocean,
Too silver for a seam—
Or Butterflies, off Banks of Noon
Leap, plashless as they swim.

AFTER great pain, a formal feeling comes—
The Nerves sit ceremonious, like Tombs—
The stiff Heart questions was it He, that bore,
And Yesterday, or Centuries before?

The Feet, mechanical, go round—
Of Ground, or Air, or Ought—
A Wooden way
Regardless grown,
A Quartz contentment, like a stone—

This is the Hour of Lead—
Remembered, if outlived,
As Freezing persons, recollect the Snow—
First—Chill—then Stupor—then the letting go—

A VISITOR in Marl—
Who influences Flowers—
Till they are orderly as Busts—
And Elegant—as Glass—

Who visits in the Night—
And just before the Sun—
Concludes his glistening interview—
Caresses—and is gone—

But whom his fingers touched—
And where his feet have run—
And whatsoever Mouth he kissed—
Is as it had not been—

WE GROW accustomed to the Dark—
When Light is put away—
As when the Neighbor holds the Lamp
To witness her Goodbye—

A Moment—We uncertain step
For newness of the night—
Then—fit our Vision to the Dark—
And meet the Road—erect—

And so of larger—Darknesses—
Those Evenings of the Brain—
When not a Moon disclose a sign—
Or Star—come out—within—

The Bravest—grope a little—
And sometimes hit a Tree
Directly in the Forehead—
But as they learn to see—

Either the Darkness alters—
Or something in the sight
Adjusts itself to Midnight—
And Life steps almost straight.

I DIED for Beauty—but was scarce
Adjusted in the Tomb
When One who died for Truth, was lain
In an adjoining Room—

He questioned softly "Why I failed"?
"For Beauty," I replied—
"And I—for Truth—Themself are One—
We Brethren, are," He said—

And so, as Kinsmen, met a Night—
We talked between the Rooms—
Until the Moss had reached our lips—
And covered up—our names—

I HEARD a Fly buzz—when I died—
The Stillness in the Room
Was like the Stillness in the Air—
Between the Heaves of Storm—

The Eyes around—had wrung them dry—
And Breaths were gathering firm
For that last Onset—when the King
Be witnessed—in the Room—

I willed my Keepsakes—Signed away
What portion of me be
Assignable—and then it was
There interposed a Fly—

With Blue—uncertain stumbling Buzz—
Between the light—and me—
And then the Windows failed—and then
I could not see to see—

I'M CEDED—I've stopped being Theirs—
The name They dropped upon my face
With water, in the country church
Is finished using, now,
And They can put it with my Dolls,
My childhood, and the string of spools,
I've finished threading—too—

Baptized, before, without the choice,
But this time, consciously, of Grace—
Unto supremest name—
Called to my Full—The Crescent dropped—
Existence's whole Arc, filled up,
With one small Diadem.

My second Rank—too small the first—
Crowned—Crowing—on my Father's breast—
A half unconscious Queen—
But this time—Adequate—Erect,
With Will to choose, or to reject,
And I choose, just a Crown—

AFTER A hundred years
Nobody knows the Place
Agony that enacted there
Motionless as Peace

Weeds triumphant ranged
Strangers strolled and spelled
At the lone Orthography
Of the Elder Dead

Winds of Summer Fields
Recollect the way—
Instinct picking up the Key
Dropped by memory—

IT WAS NOT Death, for I stood up,
And all the Dead, lie down—
It was not Night, for all the Bells
Put out their Tongues, for Noon.

It was not Frost, for on my Flesh
I felt Siroccos—crawl—
Nor Fire—for just my Marble feet
Could keep a Chancel, cool—

And yet, it tasted, like them all,
The Figures I have seen
Set orderly, for Burial,
Reminded me, of mine—

As if my life were shaven,
And fitted to a frame,
And could not breathe without a key,
And 'twas like Midnight, some—

When everything that ticked—has stopped
And Space stares all around—
Or Grisly frosts—first Autumn morns,
Repeal the Beating Ground—

But, most, like Chaos—Stopless—cool—
Without a Chance, or Spar—
Or even a Report of Land—
To justify—Despair.

I'VE SEEN a Dying Eye
Run round and round a Room—
In search of Something—as it seemed—
Then Cloudier become—
And then—obscure with Fog—
And then—be soldered down
Without disclosing what it be
'Twere blessed to have seen—

I LIKE to see it lap the Miles—
And lick the Valleys up—
And stop to feed itself at Tanks—
And then—prodigious step

Around a Pile of Mountains—
And supercilious peer
In Shanties—by the sides of Roads—
And then a Quarry pare

To fit its Ribs
And crawl between
Complaining all the while
In horrid—hooting stanza—
Then chase itself down Hill

And neigh like Boanerges—
Then—punctual as a Star
Stop—docile and omnipotent
At its own stable door—

THE BRAIN—is wider than the Sky—
For—put them side by side—
The one the other will contain
With ease—and You—beside—

The Brain is deeper than the sea—
For—hold them—Blue to Blue—
The one the other will absorb—
As Sponges—Buckets—do—

The Brain is just the weight of God—
For—Heft them—Pound for Pound—
And they will differ—if they do—
As Syllable from Sound—

I CANNOT live with You—
It would be Life—
And Life is over there—
Behind the Shelf

The Sexton keeps the Key to—
Putting up
Our Life—His Porcelain—
Like a Cup—

Discarded of the Housewife—
Quaint—or Broke—
A newer Sevres pleases—
Old Ones crack—

I could not die—with You—
For One must wait
To shut the Other's Gaze down—
You—could not—

And I—Could I stand by
And see You—freeze—
Without my Right of Frost—
Death's privilege?

Nor could I rise—with You—
Because Your Face
Would put out Jesus'—
That New Grace

Glow plain—and foreign
On my homesick Eye—
Except that You than He
Shone closer by—

They'd judge Us—How—
For You—served Heaven—You know,
Or sought to—
I could not—

Because You saturated Sight—
And I had no more Eyes
For sordid excellence
As Paradise

And were You lost, I would be—
Though My Name
Rang loudest
On the Heavenly fame—

BESIDES the Autumn poets sing
A few prosaic days
A little this side of the snow
And that side of the Haze—

A few incisive Mornings—
A few Ascetic Eyes—
Gone—Mr. Bryant's "Golden Rod"—
And Mr. Thomson's "sheaves."

Still, is the bustle in the Brook—
Sealed are the spicy valves—
Mesmeric fingers softly touch
The Eyes of many Elves—

Perhaps a squirrel may remain—
My sentiments to share—
Grant me, Oh Lord, a sunny mind—
Thy windy will to bear!

EACH LIFE Converges to some Centre—
Expressed—or still—
Exists in every Human Nature
A Goal—

Embodied scarcely to itself—it may be—
Too fair
For Credibility's presumption
To mar—

Adored with caution—as a Brittle Heaven—
To reach
Were hopeless, as the Rainbow's Raiment
To touch—

Yet persevered toward—sure—for the Distance—
How high—
Unto the Saints' slow diligence—
The Sky—

Ungained—it may be—by a Life's low Venture—
But then—
Eternity enable the endeavoring
Again.

THE SOUL selects her own Society—
Then—shuts the Door—
To her divine Majority—
Present no more—

Unmoved—she notes the Chariots—pausing—
At her low Gate—
Unmoved—an Emperor be kneeling
Upon her Mat—

I've known her—from an ample nation—
Choose One—
Then—close the Valves of her attention—
Like Stone—

BECAUSE I could not stop for Death—
He kindly stopped for me—
The Carriage held but just Ourselves—
And Immortality.

We slowly drove—He knew no haste
And I had put away
My labor and my leisure too,
For His Civility—

We passed the School, where Children strove
At Recess—in the Ring—
We passed the Fields of Gazing Grain—
We passed the Setting Sun—

Or rather—He passed Us—
The Dews drew quivering and chill—
For only Gossamer, my Gown—
My Tippet—only Tulle—

We paused before a House that seemed
A Swelling of the Ground—
The Roof was scarcely visible—
The Cornice—in the Ground—

Since then—'tis Centuries—and yet
Feels shorter than the Day
I first surmised the Horses' Heads
Were toward Eternity—

THIS QUIET Dust was Gentlemen and Ladies
And Lads and Girls—
And laughter and ability and Sighing
And Frocks and Curls.

This Passive Place a Summer's nimble mansion
Where Bloom and Bees
Exists an Oriental Circuit
Then cease, like these—

THE WIND begun to rock the Grass
With threatening Tunes and low—
He threw a Menace at the Earth—
A Menace at the Sky.

The Leaves unhooked themselves from Trees—
And started all abroad
The Dust did scoop itself like Hands
And threw away the Road.

The Wagons quickened on the Streets
The Thunder hurried slow—
The Lightning showed a Yellow Beak
And then a livid Claw.

The Birds put up the Bars to Nests—
The Cattle fled to Barns—
There came one drop of Giant Rain
And then as if the Hands

That held the Dams had parted hold
The Waters Wrecked the Sky,
But overlooked my Father's House—
Just quartering a Tree—

IT SIFTS from Leaden Sieves—
It powders all the Wood.
It fills with Alabaster Wool
The Wrinkles of the Road—

It makes an Even Face
Of Mountain, and of Plain—
Unbroken Forehead from the East
Unto the East again—

It reaches to the Fence—
It wraps it Rail by Rail
Till it is lost in Fleeces—
It deals Celestial Vail

To Stump, and Stack   and Stem—
A Summer's empty Room—
Acres of Joints, where Harvests were,
Recordless, but for them—

It Ruffles Wrists of Posts
As Ankles of a Queen—
Then stills its Artisans—like Ghosts—
Denying they have been—

IT SOUNDED as if the Streets were running
And then—the Streets stood still—
Eclipse—was all we could see at the Window
And Awe—was all we could feel.

By and by—the boldest stole out of his Covert
To see if Time was there—
Nature was in an Opal Apron,
Mixing fresher Air.

I DREADED that first Robin, so,
But He is mastered, now,
I'm some accustomed to Him grown,
He hurts a little, though—

I thought if I could only live
Till that first Shout got by—
Not all Pianos in the Woods
Had power to mangle me—

I dared not meet the Daffodils—
For fear their Yellow Gown
Would pierce me with a fashion
So foreign to my own—

I wished the Grass would hurry—
So—when 'twas time to see—
He'd be too tall, the tallest one
Could stretch—to look at me—

I could not bear the Bees should come,
I wished they'd stay away
In those dim countries where they go,
What word had they, for me?

They're here, though; not a creature failed—
No Blossom stayed away
In gentle deference to me—
The Queen of Calvary—

Each one salutes me, as he goes,
And I, my childish Plumes,
Lift, in bereaved acknowledgment
Of their unthinking Drums—

A ROUTE of Evanescence
With a revolving Wheel—
A Resonance of Emerald—
A Rush of Cochineal—
And every Blossom on the Bush
Adjusts its tumbled Head—
The mail from Tunis, probably,
An easy Morning's Ride—

MY LIFE closed twice before its close—
It yet remains to see
If Immortality unveil
A third event to me

So huge, so hopeless to conceive
As these that twice befell.
Parting is all we know of heaven,
And all we need of hell.

A NARROW Fellow in the Grass
Occasionally rides—
You may have met Him—did you not
His notice sudden is—

The Grass divides as with a Comb—
A spotted shaft is seen—
And then it closes at your feet
And opens further on—

He likes a Boggy Acre
A Floor too cool for Corn—
Yet when a Boy, and Barefoot—
I more than once at Noon

Have passed, I thought, a Whip lash
Unbraiding in the Sun
When stooping to secure it
It wrinkled, and was gone—

Several of Nature's People
I know, and they know me—
I feel for them a transport
Of cordiality—

But never met this Fellow
Attended, or alone
Without a tighter breathing
And Zero at the Bone—

TELL ALL the Truth but tell it slant—
Success in Circuit lies
Too bright for our infirm Delight
The Truth's superb surprise
As Lightning to the Children eased
With explanation kind
The Truth must dazzle gradually
Or every man be blind—

AS IMPERCEPTIBLY as Grief
The Summer lapsed away—
Too imperceptible at last
To seem like Perfidy—
A Quietness distilled
As Twilight long begun,
Or Nature spending with herself
Sequestered Afternoon—
The Dusk drew earlier in—
The Morning foreign shone—
A courteous, yet harrowing Grace,
As Guest, that would be gone—
And thus, without a Wing
Or service of a Keel
Our Summer made her light escape
Into the Beautiful.

THE BUSTLE in a House
The Morning after Death
Is solemnest of industries
Enacted upon Earth—

The Sweeping up the Heart
And putting Love away
We shall not want to use again
Until Eternity.

ELYSIUM IS as far as to
The very nearest Room
If in that Room a Friend await
Felicity or Doom—

What fortitude the Soul contains,
That it can so endure
The accent of a coming Foot—
The opening of a Door—

I SHALL keep singing!
Birds will pass me
On their way to Yellower Climes—
Each—with a Robin's expectation—
I—with my Redbreast—
And my Rhymes—

Late—when I take my place in summer—
But—I shall bring a fuller tune—
Vespers—are sweeter than Matins—Signor—
Morning—only the seed of Noon—

Afterword

One of Emily Dickinson's best biographers, Richard Chase, has said that out of her hundreds upon hundreds of poems he supposed perhaps fifty are excellent and among those fifty perhaps a dozen or two are great. It would be an arrogant editor who could assume he had put his finger on the very poems that constitute her best, but it would be an exaggeratedly humble editor who did not try.

We know from Thomas H. Johnson's complete editions of Emily Dickinson—presumably final and unquestionably superb—that she left us a total of 1,775 poems. Seven were published in her lifetime—often as not, revised to more conventional phraseology and rhyming by well-meaning (that is to say, insensitive) editors. So Emily's poetic career is posthumous. She dropped many poems into letters to friends and relatives, but nobody seems to have had any conception of the extent to which she wrote; not even her sister Lavinia, who discovered, saved and promoted publication of the poems after Emily's death; not even her principal literary correspondent, Thomas Wentworth Higginson. No; there was never anybody to tell little Emily Dickinson that she stood tall in the front rank of American poets—that, indeed, she had written greater poems than any other woman in all literature.

If we ask how this triumph came about we shall ask mostly in vain. Yet we can sense a nearness of approach to Emily Dickinson as a woman if we bear in mind that in many ways her sparse biography reveals her as a type. In New England throughout the 19th and on into the 20th century there were countless spinsters who lived out their lives in their fathers' houses, who cooked and baked and gardened and did other household chores, who were seldom seen about the town and became more solitary and eccentric with the years, and wound up caring for a long-invalided parent; they accentuated the maiden aunt's life that so poignantly often gave more love than it received. Emily Dickinson's difference is that she had genius.

She was born in Amherst, Massachusetts, on the 10th of December, 1830, in her Grandfather Dickinson's fine brick house which still stands on Main Street. From Emily's tenth to twenty-fifth year her family—father, mother, brother Austin and the two sisters—lived in a house on Pleasant Street; but in 1855 her father reclaimed the family mansion. There Emily Dickinson's poems were written and it was there she died, aged 55, on the 15th of May, 1886. It is a haunted shrine.

Emily's mother seems to have been colorlessly domestic, but her father, Edward Dickinson, was the strong archetype of the Puritan-descended Yankee: lawyer, Congressman, zealous associate of Amherst College, and unsmiling, unbending, righteous and honorable, not very approachable—the Father as Victorian God. There is evidence the Dickinsons were considered, and thought themselves to be, rather above most people in Amherst. Though as to that, they never knew their best reason for thinking so.

Several times in her young life Emily Dickinson made visits to relatives' homes in and around Boston, the last when she was not quite 35. As a girl she unsuccessfully ventured a year at nearby South Hadley, attending Mount Holyoke Female Seminary. Once in her early twenties she accompanied her family to Washington, D.C., and Philadelphia. Otherwise she remained in Amherst, and from her mid-thirties until her death she stayed so exclusively within her home itself that very few people ever saw her. Her only photograph looks like a deer about to turn and flee. One of those who saw her—Higginson, on two occasions—has left us invaluable records of the small, plain woman "with two smooth bands of reddish hair." Higginson concluded: "I never was with anyone who drained my nerve power so much .... I am glad not to live near her."

Was there one man who might have been glad to? Or, more probably, one man whom Emily Dickinson loved but who was married and did not return her love? A man renounced in many poems, especially at her overwhelming tide of creativity in the early 1860's when some great crisis of her life terrified her, and in her subsequent reclusion? If there was a particular man, coordination of poems, letters and biographical data seems to indicate Samuel Bowles, editor of the *Springfield Republican.*

"Heaven is what I cannot reach," she writes. She rephrases this over and over in her work. She is the poet of renunciation, the poet of non-possession. She is a skeptical poet. Fond of speaking of Immortality and Eternity, she is apt to conclude "if true," apt to glance at "that old codicil of doubt." She is obsessed with change as all her life she observes the comings and goings of flowers, birds, insects, of seasons, and of human beings and their finalities. All these in her immediate world: perhaps it is the least of Emily Dickinson's achievement, yet shouldn't we note that her *Complete Poems* belongs in its way with the supreme small-town books of American literature? However she transcends merely that, nonetheless she demonstrates yet again how the local can become the universal.

To read all the 1,775 poems as a continuous stint is a stupifying experience. She is seen and heard most clearly in small doses—as in such a slender book as this. Much of her work founders. She can be coy, lisping, mawkish, sentimental in her moods of "God, I'm just a little girl." Also, with her steel needle of a mind, she can cram her thought to pithy comment, to epigram and aphorism, to an almost imageless verse which fails of itself. Yet in many of her lesser poems there are unforgettable flashes.

Here we move toward her excellence. Poetry has no deeper essence than concentration of language, and precisely in this Emily Dickinson takes her place with the very great. As did her physical presence to Higginson, so her poems demand much of us. The reward is commensurate. When we give her the attention she requires we find we begin to give her love. We learn to delight in the impact of impacted language, in the gnomic phrasing, the fresh and startling imagery, in the very odd "rhyming" that somehow is a part of the awesome integrity, of the fiery necessity to speak truth. Her poems are perhaps the vividest evidence that the poet need not go everywhere, see everything, live widely, to make great art. Great art arises from being so intensely alive where the artist is, even in the confines of a single house and yard. Exterior security can contain interior drama and even in a New England mansion provide infinite supplies of agony and bliss.

W.T. S.